501
Great
Kiwi
Jokes

501 Great Kiwi Jokes

PROUDLY SUPPORTING

TURNING RESEARCH INTO HOPE

SCHOLASTIC
AUCKLAND SYDNEY NEW YORK LONDON TORONTO
MEXICO CITY NEW DELHI HONG KONG

First published in 2011 by Scholastic New Zealand Limited
Private Bag 94407, Botany, Auckland 2163, New Zealand

Scholastic Australia Pty Limited
PO Box 579, Gosford, NSW 2250, Australia

This collection © Scholastic NZ Ltd New Zealand Limited, 2011

ISBN 978-1-77543-035-3

National Library of New Zealand Cataloguing-in-Publication Data

501 great kiwi jokes / [illustrations by Donovan Bixley].
ISBN 978-1-77543-035-3
1.Wit and humor, Juvenile. 2. Riddles, Juvenile.
3. New Zealand wit and humor—21st century.
[1. Jokes. 2. Riddles.]
I. Bixley, Donovan. II. Title.
NZ828.30208—dc 22

12 11 10 9 8 7 6 5 4   6 7 8 9 / 1

Illustrations by Donovan Bixley
Special thanks to contributor Leah Brooks
Publishing team: Diana Murray, Penny Scown and Annette Bisman
Designer: Book Design Ltd
Typeset in Minya Nouvelle by Book Design Ltd www.bookdesign.co.nz
Printed in Malaysia by Tien Wah Press (PTE) Ltd

Scholastic New Zealand's policy, in association with Tien Wah Press, is to use papers
that are renewable and made efficiently from wood grown in sustainable forests, so as to
minimise its environmental footprint.

TURNING RESEARCH INTO HOPE

About Cure Kids

Cure Kids is committed to funding vital medical research into life-threatening childhood illnesses. Here at Cure Kids we are proud of our primary objective, which is to fund innovative, results-driven research that brings hope to children and families throughout New Zealand.

Over the years Cure Kids has funded research advancements in diseases such as childhood leukaemia, long QT syndrome, cystic fibrosis, cot death, genetic research, and severe asthma. Cure Kids is unique in that, as part of our mission to find cures, we fully believe in having fun to raise those all important funds!

As we turn research into hope, we love to put a smile on a child's face – after all, it's all about the kids.

www.curekids.co.nz

FOREWORD

At Cure Kids we believe in giving children who live with an illness the opportunity to step back and just enjoy life. Every year we take many of these amazing children on a 'Ticket to Hope' and they have that all-important opportunity to laugh, have fun and, perhaps, just feel like a normal kid for one weekend.

Having fun raising funds is our unique way of involving the community and businesses into this very important cause. From outdoor events that challenge the body and soul to fun campaigns, Cure Kids passionately believes in working together to seriously give our children hope. It's truly moving to see so many people put so much time and effort into raising money for the sole aim of improving the quality of life of Kiwi children facing major health issues every day — and seeing our Ambassadors at the finish line is truly inspiring!

We have already made world-first medical breakthroughs with the amazing researchers that we fund — and we are on a mission to make many more. **With your support** of this fantastic Kiwi Joke Book you are helping thousands of Kiwi kids by simply having a good old laugh.

Vicki Lee
CEO, Cure Kids

Contents

Kiwi Crack-Ups

What kind of letters do you send
to Wellington?
Capital letters.

What's in the middle of Dunedin?
The letter E!

Billy: How do you make a mattamate?
Jack: What's a mattamate?
Billy: Nothing, mate. What's a matter
with you?

Where in New Zealand do the most people
with curly hair live?
Frizz-borne!

What city do The Three Little Pigs avoid?
Ham-ilton!

What do kiwi, weta, tuatara
and kea have in common?
They have a birthday
every year!

One day Tom looked over his fence and
saw his neighbour, Barry, throwing big
handfuls of white powder all over his
front lawn.

'What are you doing?' asked Tom.

'Well,' said Barry, 'I bought this powder
from a man at the market. He said that if
I spread it all over my lawn it would keep
all the gorillas away!'

'But Barry,' said Tom, 'there aren't any
gorillas around here!'

'I know,' answered Barry. 'Pretty good,
isn't it?'

Which New Zealand island makes the
best casseroles?
Stew-art Island!

Where did the card player go when he was
dealt a bad hand?
Bluff!

Where do New Zealand mosquitoes live?
Mozz-giel!

Why did the chicken cross the A&P Show?
To get to the other ride!

How do you get rid of a fly?
Tell it to buzz off!

Which New Zealand town
is most unforgeta-bull?
Bulls!

Where did the Kiwi baker go when she retired?
Pie-roa!

What does a kauri tree do when it's ready to go home?
It leaves!

What often falls in the South Island but never gets hurt?
Snow!

Why did the bungy jumper take a holiday?
Because he was at the end of his rope.

What does New Zealand produce that no other country produces?
New Zealanders!

Where do Meals on Wheels come from?
Kai-tyre!

Where do you go to weigh a pie?
Somewhere, over the rainbow, weigh a pie!

Jack is standing on the door step watching Scott put out the rubbish.

As Scott goes by he yells out to Jack, 'Hey bro, where's your bin?'

Jack replies, 'I bin in Australia.'

'No,' replies Scott, 'where's your wheelie bin?'

'Oh, I wheelie bin in jail, but I tell people I bin in Australia!'

Sweet-As Sport

What can you serve but never eat?
A tennis ball!

What do you get if you cross a skunk and
a pair of tennis rackets?
Ping pong!

What flavour chips does the New Zealand
gymnastics team eat?
Somersault and vinegar!

Why was the chickens' soccer match a
bad idea?
Because there were too many fowls.

When is a baby good at basketball?
When it dribbles!

What has two wings but cannot fly?
A rugby team.

What illness do martial artists get?
Kung Flu.

How do Kiwi cricketers stay cool?
They sit next to their fans.

What goes all
around a cricket
oval but never moves?
The boundary line.

What do runners do when they forget
something?
They jog their memory.

Why was the Kiwi athlete so easy to get
along with?
Because he was always willing
to discus things!

Why are goalkeepers
always the wealthiest?
They really know
how to save.

What kind of football do you play
without boots?
Socker.

What's the difference between a cricketer
and a dog?
The cricketer has a complete uniform,
but the dog only pants!

Did you hear about the Kiwi champion who
broke her ankle while tap dancing?
She fell into the sink.

Why did the golfer take two pairs of
pants to the game?
In case he got a hole in one!

What sport do photographers play?
Clickit.

Why did the Kiwi golfer have to
walk home?
He couldn't find his driver.

Did you hear about the Kiwi golfer who
forced a canary to play a shot for him?
He made a birdie putt.

When do Kiwi
golfers drive off?
Tee time.

Foodie Fun

What's a sheep's favourite
thing to eat?
A baaaanana.

How do bakers swap recipes?
On a knead to dough basis.

Store owner: Good morning Janet! What
can I get for you?
Janet: Something for dinner, please.
Store owner: I have some lovely fresh ox
tongue.
Janet: Oh, no! Yuck! I couldn't eat something
that comes out of an animal's mouth! I'll
have a dozen eggs.

Which vegetable loves athletics?
Runner bean.

Which vegetable is always a bit damp?
Leek.

Which vegetable has been in a fight?
Black-eyed pea!

What did one plate say to the other?
Lunch is on me!

Which fruit goes around in twos?
Pears!

In the old days, what did you call
fast food?
Food you couldn't catch!

Why do the French eat snails?
Because they like slow food!

A guy sits alone in a hotel lounge one night enjoying a quiet drink when he suddenly hears a voice ...

'Nice shirt.'

He looks around but there's no-one else in the room except for the waiter way up the other end. He puts the voice down to a long week in the office and goes back to his drink. A minute later he hears the voice again ...

'Nice tie, goes well with the suit. Is it Italian?'

The guy spins around, looks up and down the place but again, there's no one to be seen but the waiter, polishing glasses down the far end. He turns back to his drink and once again ...

'I like your haircut, pal. Very sharp.'

The guy is starting to worry for his sanity and calls to the waiter, 'Excuse me mate, are you talking to me?'

'No,' replies the waiter. 'Why?'

'I just keep hearing this voice saying nice things to me,' says the guy.

'Oh, that'd be the peanuts,' says the waiter. 'They're complimentary.'

What happened when the butcher backed up to his meat grinder?
He got a little behind in his work.

What do you call a sad strawberry?
A blueberry.

Which fruit keeps hedges neat?
Prune.

How do you make a sausage roll?
Push it!

Why did the tomato turn red?
It saw the salad dressing!

Judge: Order in the court!
Convict: I'll have a hamburger and fries.

What do you call a bloke you have
to pay after you've finished eating at
a restaurant?
Bill.

Where do parents keep the baby food?
In the mush-room.

A family of three tomatoes is walking
downtown one day when the little baby
tomato starts lagging behind. The big
father tomato walks back to the baby
tomato, stomps on her, squashing her into
a red paste, and says, 'Ketchup!'

Mum: Marama, eat your puha!
It's good for growing children.
Marama: But I don't want
to grow any children!

A banana walks into a
doctor's office and the
doctor asks her what's wrong.
The banana says, 'I don't peel so good.'

What did the pun say to the egg?
Is this a yolk?

How do code-breakers like their eggs?
Scrambled.

Why didn't the hot dog act in the play?
The roll wasn't good enough.

Billy: What's the special today?
Waiter: It's bean soup.
Billy: Yes, but what is it now?

A bloke goes to a bakery that specialises in crazy-shaped bread. There are loaves shaped like kiwi and kauri and cars. He buys one that looks like a chess-board and takes it home. But when he goes to make a sandwich he finds that his new loaf of bread is as hard as a rock, so he takes it back to the bakery.

When the baker asks why he's bringing it back, he replies, 'It's stale, mate.'

The baker doesn't believe him and refuses to return his money. So the bloke shows the loaf to the baker and says, 'Check, mate!'

A lady went into a butcher shop complaining about the sausages she had just bought. 'The middle is meat,' she exclaimed, 'but the ends are sawdust!'

'Well,' said the butcher, 'these days it's hard to make ends meat.'

What's red and goes up and down?
A tomato in a lift!

Why did the elephant sit
on the marshmallow?
So she wouldn't fall into
the hot chocolate.

Which fruit is always breaking down?
Lemon!

What do you get when you ask a lemon
for help?
Lemon-aid.

What's grumpy and goes really well with
ice cream?
Apple grumble.

What did the rabbit say to the carrot?
It's been nice gnawing you!

Why are tomatoes round and red?
Because if they were long and yellow,
they'd be bananas!

Did you hear about the poor bloke who
arranged for home-delivered fish 'n' chips
then forgot where he'd ordered them?
He didn't know where his next meal was
coming from.

What food is hard to beat for breakfast?
A boiled egg.

What is orange and sounds like a parrot?
A carrot.

Why did the bacon laugh?
Because the egg cracked a yolk!

Awesome Animal Antics

Why did the dairy farmer ride his horse?
Because it was too heavy to carry!

Why did the tuatara
cross the road?
It was following
the chicken.

Why did the tuatara
cross the road again?
It was a double-crosser.

What do you call a bloke with a seagull
on his head?
Cliff.

What's an Archey's frog's favourite drink?
Croak-a-Cola!

Why did the kiwi sit on the clock?
So she could be on time!

What sound do hedgehogs make when
they kiss?
Ouch!

Why did the weta climb over the glass wall?
To see what was on the other side!

How do catch a unique fantail?
U-nique up on him!

How do you catch a tame fantail?
Tame way.

Why did the pukeko cross
the road?
To prove he wasn't a chicken!

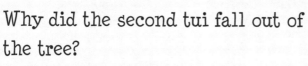

Why did the tui fall
out of the tree?
Because it was dead.

Why did the second tui fall out of
the tree?
It was hit by the first one.

Why did the third tui fall out of the tree?
It thought it was a game and joined in.

Who delivers presents to young mako
sharks at Christmas?
Santa Jaws!

What do kereru use for napkins?
Flapkins!

What happens when a kuri and a giraffe
cross paths?
Broken legs!

What do you call a dog that's disappeared?
A doggone.

What type of umbrella would a pukeko
have on a rainy day?
A wet one!

Why did the freezing seagull fly onto the
telephone line?
It wanted to chatter!

What did the snapper say when it swam
into the wall?
Dam!

Which animal can jump
higher than Mount Everest?
a)   Kiri Kiwi
b)   Archey Frog
c)   Marama Morepork
Any of the above, because
mountains can't jump!

Why did the tui fall
out of the tree?
He was asleep.

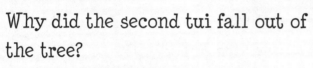

Why did the second tui fall out of
the tree?
He was stapled to the first tui.

Why did the third tui fall out of the tree?
Peer pressure.

What did the hedgehog say to the cactus?
Are you my mother?

Where do sheep go to get a haircut?
The baa-baa's!

What do you get when you cross a frog
with a sheep?
A woolly jumper!

What do you call a field of giggling cows?
Laughing stock.

Why did the dairy farmer take his cow to
the psychiatrist?
Because she was moooody.

Why couldn't the bee contact his friend
on the phone?
He kept getting a buzzy signal.

What do you get when your dog has its
sixth birthday?
A six-year-old dog.

Music Mayhem

Why did Kiri break into song?
Because she couldn't find a key.

What kind of music
does your father
like to play?
Pop music.

What instrument do elephants play?
The trumpet!

What's a chicken's favourite instrument?
Cluckstanets.

What is it called when a person sings in the shower?
A soap opera.

What part of the turkey is musical?
The drumstick!

How do you make a bandstand?
Hide all their chairs!

Why do some rock'n'roll bands wreck the platforms they play on?
It's just a stage they go through!

What do you call a fish musician?
Piano tuna.

What do you get when you drop a piano down a mineshaft?
A flat minor.

What do you get when you drop a piano on an army base?
A flat major.

What do you say to an army officer just as you are about to run him over with a steam roller?
B flat, major.

What is a sailor's favourite musical note?
C flat.

How do you fix a broken tuba?
With a tuba glue.

Which famous composer always leaned to one side?
Liszt!

Which famous composer could never be found?
Haydn.

What's the difference between a fish
and a piano?
You can't tuna fish.

Why couldn't the athlete listen to
her music?
Because she broke the record.

What makes music on your head?
A head band.

Why did the girl sit on a ladder to sing?
She wanted to reach the high notes.

Hard Case Laughs

What happened to the burglar who stole a calendar?
He got a full twelve months.

What happened to the burglar who fell and broke his leg in wet cement?
He became a hardened criminal.

Why were the police called to the daycare centre?
Because a three-year-old needed a rest.

Did you hear about the guy whose left side was cut off?
He's all right now.

What do you call a man
holding a shovel?
Doug.

What do you call a man who
doesn't have a shovel?
Douglas.

What did one ear say to the other ear?
Between you and me, we need a haircut.

What has four legs and doesn't walk?
A table.

What did the stamp say to the envelope?
Stick with me and we'll go places.

Can a match box?
No, but a tin can.

Why did the weatherman quit?
Because the climate didn't agree with him!

How do you make a hot-dog stand?
Steal its chair.

Why did the man sleep under the car?
So he could wake up oily in the morning.

What does a clock do when it's hungry?
It goes back four seconds!

What happened to the guy who
fell onto an upholstery machine?
He fully recovered!

What's brown and sticky?
A stick.

Two hats were hanging on a hat rack in
the hallway.

One hat said to the other, 'you stay here,
I'll go on a head.'

A doctor, a lawyer and an accountant walk into a restaurant and the waiter says, 'What is this? A joke?'

What did the New Zealand flag say to the pole?
Nothing, it just waved.

Why don't pirates have headache pills?
Because the parrots-eat-'em-all.

Where do Kiwi generals keep their armies?
Up their sleevies!

Hotel receptionist: How did you sleep?
Guest: Like a baby.
Hotel receptionist: You woke up crying every two hours with a wet nappy?

What is a baby's motto?
If at first you don't succeed, cry, cry again!

What award did the inventor of the doorknocker win?
The No-Bell prize.

Janet: My little girl Suzy is only two, but she's been walking since she was nine months old!
Tracey: She must be very tired ...

How do you join the Royal New Zealand Navy?
Handcuff all the sailors together.

What did the Vikings use to send secret messages?
Norse code.

Why are computers always so tired when they get home?
Because they all have hard drives!

How do you make a woolly jumper
with a computer?
Use the interknit.

What's the difference
between a Kiwi lighthouse
keeper, a watchmaker and
a tube of superglue?
One watches the seas and
the other sees the watches.

What about the tube of superglue?
Well, that's where you get stuck!

Why did Billy put spectacles on his dad's
timber saw?
He wanted a see-saw!

What colour answers the phone?
Yellow.

Little Jack: Dad! Can I have another glass of water?
Dad: But I've given you nine glasses already! Are you really that thirsty?
Little Jack: No! My bedroom's still on fire!

If a red house is made of red bricks and a blue house is made of blue bricks, what is a green house made out of?
Glass.

Which months have 28 days?
All of them!

Why do you always find things in the last place you look?
Because after you find it, you stop looking!

Why was the full stop set free?
It had finished its sentence.

What did the zero say to the eight at
the party?
Nice belt.

What kind of clothes do aquariums wear?
Tank tops!

Did you hear about the photographer who
lost his temper?
He snapped!

What are the last things New Zealanders
take off before going to bed?
Their feet off the floor.

Can a book change colour?
Yes. If it's not red when
you begin reading it,
it'll be red when
you've finished.

Did you hear about the cardboard woman
who resigned?
She felt she wasn't cut out for the job.

Why did the dishwasher fear he'd drown?
Because he felt the kitchen sink!

Which plant loves being fired?
Rocket.

Which plant is useful for washing the dishes?
Bottlebrush.

What does the man say when he walks
into a bar?
Ouch!

Which plant loves to be part of a blizzard?
Snowdrop.

Which tree looks neat and tidy?
Spruce.

Which tree is well-liked by all the
other trees?
Poplar.

Which tree is full of sand?
Beech.

Did you hear about James, the hungry
16-year-old?
He eight and eight.

Did you hear about Sarah, the hungry
32-year-old?
She eight and eight and eight and eight.

Why were the fern and the palm happy
to see each other?
They were old fronds.

What did the digital clock
 say to the analogue clock?
Look ma, no hands!

What kind of shoes do spies wear?
Sneakers!

What do you call a bloke who walks
in leaves?
Russell.

Why did the pirate look in the dictionary?
To see how to spell 'R'!

What do trees drink?
Root beer.

What is famous artist
Kiri Kiwi's favourite line?
Do you get the picture?

Why did Kiri Kiwi put lipstick on
her head?
Because she was trying to make-up
her mind!

What did the coat hanger say to the shirt?
Do you have to hang around me all day?

What do you call a computer superhero?
A screensaver!

Why do Komodo dragons sleep all day?
So that they can stay up and fight knights!

What do you call a bloke who is always
stealing things?
Rob.

Why did the cops wake up the
sleeping child?
They heard that there was a kid napping.

What's the difference between Sharon the
jeweller and Aaron the jailer?
One sells watches and the other watches
cells!

One day Bazza decides that he's had enough of working and decides to become a thief. He goes out and snatches a purse from the first lady he sees. Unfortunately, Bazza is so dim that he does it in front of a policeman and the cop chases him. Bazza runs away down an alley, and the policeman follows. At the end of the alley the policeman sees that it is a dead end and there is nothing there but three large sacks.

That Bazza must be hiding in one of them, thinks the policeman and pokes the first sack with his boot.

'Grr-Woof!' comes a noise from the sack. There is a dog hiding inside.

'Meee-oww!' comes the noise from the second sack. Cats, thinks the policeman. He moves on to the third sack and pokes it with his boot.

At first, there is silence. Then, 'Aaah ... umm ... potatoes?'

What happened when the police found Jack, the little lost boy, hiding under a blanket?

There was a cover-up.

Pessimist: My glass is half empty.
Optimist: My glass is half full.
Detective: Dust the glass for prints and find out who's been drinking my L&P!

Why did the scarecrow win so many awards?

Because he was outstanding in his field.

Around the World

What did the volcano say to his girlfriend?
I lava you.

What do you call a chicken in Antarctica?
Lost!

What else do you call a chicken in Antarctica?
Cold!

Which ancient city never stays still?
Roam.

Ella: Our new neighbours are Irish!
Ben: Oh, really?
Ella: No, O'Reilly.

Which country has the most microbes?
Germ-any!

Which country is the best at board games?
Checkerslovakia!

Which country has the worst singers?
Sing-a-poor!

William: I took my wife on holiday to
the Caribbean.
Henare: Jamaica?
William: No, she wanted to go!

Which country has the chilliest people?
Brrrrrazil!

Which country eats the most tinned fruit?
Can-ada!

Which country is always dressed smartly?
Tie-land!

There are two snowmen standing on a hill. One turns to the other and says, 'Say, do you smell carrots?'

How do you make a Venetian blind?
Poke him in the eye.

Which country has the most pirates?
Arrr-gentina!

Which country has the most church bells?
Bell-gium!

If a green bloke runs over the Southern Alps, what does he become?
Tired!

What does a Spanish farmer say to his hens?
Olé!

What's the smartest mountain in the world?
Mount Cleverest.

Why can't Egyptian swimmers face
up to the truth?
They're mostly in de Nile.

Did you hear the joke about the Inuit
people at the North Pole?
Don't worry; it would chill you to
the bone!

What did the Kiwi tourist say to the
Inuit about his new igloo?
That's an ice house you have there!

What is the best thing to take into
the Sahara Desert?
A thirst aid kit!

Why is Europe like a
frying pan?
Because it has Greece
at the bottom.

Ghostly Guffaws

Why did the zombie decide to stay in his coffin?
He felt rotten.

How can you tell an alien would be a good gardener?
They have green thumbs.

What music do ghosts dance to?
Soul music.

What do you get if you cross a snowman and a vampire?
Frostbite.

Why are graveyards so noisy?
Because of all the coffin.

How do you make a witch itch?
Take away the W.

What kind of ape likes New Zealand
horror movies?
A gore-illa.

How do ghosts like their eggs in the morning?
Terrifried.

How do ghosts style their hair?
Scare spray.

Why do ghosts go to parties?
To have a wail of a time.

What's a ghost's favourite musical?
My Fear Lady.

What does one ghost say to the other?
Don't spook until you're spooken to.

What does a ghost do when he gets in
the car?
Puts his sheet belt on.

Why are ghosts so bad at lying?
Because you can see right through them.

What do you get when you cross
a teacher with a vampire?
Lots of blood tests!

What do you call a vampire
who lives in your kitchen
utensils drawer?
Count Spatula!

What kind of dog is the scariest?
The terror-ier.

What day did the bloke turn into a werewolf?
Moonday.

What day did the werewolf start eating
people?
Chewsday.

What day did the werewolf turn back
into a bloke?
Mensday.

What day did the bloke find hair
everywhere from when he was a werewolf?
Fursday.

What day did the bloke decide to have
bacon and eggs instead of becoming a
werewolf again?
Fryday.

Why did the pilot scream in terror?
He got a terrible flight.

Why did the priest take the ghost for a walk?

He was asked to exorcise it.

Why didn't James the skeleton jump off the building?

He had no guts.

What did Sarah the skeleton say to the other skeleton before dinner?

Bone appetit!

Why did James the skeleton go to the music shop?

To get a new organ.

What is a little witch's best subject at school?

Spell-ing.

How did the little witch know what time
to go to school?
She looked at her witchwatch.

What do near-sighted ghosts use to read?
Spookticles.

What does Barbie the skeleton have
for dinner?
Some ribs.

What do you call a skeleton that's always
late for school?
Lazy bones.

What do you get if you cross a phone
with a ghost?
A phantom phone booth.

What is a ghost's favourite animal?
A night-mare!

What are a ghost's scariest camp-fire stories?
Human stories!

What do you get when you cross a
werewolf with a dozen eggs?
A very hairy omelette.

What are the symptoms of vampire flu?
Lots of coffin.

What do you get if you cross a dinosaur
with a ghost?
A boo-saurus.

What do you get if you cross a ghost with
a vacuum cleaner?
A howler!

What do vampires cross the sea in?
Blood vessels.

More Awesome Animal Antics

What do you get when you cross a cat with a platypus?
A platypuss.

What do you call a platypus trapped under a rock?
A flatypus!

What goes black, white, black, white, black, white?
A zebra stuck in a revolving door.

What do cats put in soft drinks?
Mice cubes.

How do you fit four elephants into a Mini?
Two in the front, two in the back.

How do you fit four giraffes into a Mini?
There's no room. It's full of elephants.

How can you tell if there's an elephant in
your refrigerator?
The milk smells like peanuts.

How can you tell if there are two elephants
in your refrigerator?
They always giggle when the light goes out.

How can you tell if there are three
elephants in your refrigerator?
You can't close the door.

How can you tell if there are four
elephants in your refrigerator?
There's a Mini parked outside.

How can you fit a dinosaur
into a Mini?
It doesn't matter,
the elephants
were there first!

What do you call a donkey with three legs?
A wonky donkey!

What do you call a donkey with three legs
and one eye?
A winky wonky donkey!

There are two monkeys in a bath.
One says 'ooo ooo ooo'. The other says,
'If it's too hot, put some cold in!'

What do you call a woodpecker with no beak?
A headbanger.

What do you give a dog with a fever?
Mustard. (It's good for a hot dog.)

What kind of monkey can fly?
A hot-air baboon.

What do you call a camel with three humps?
Humphrey.

What do you use to get antlers to grow
out of your hair?
Moose.

What goes cluck, cluck, cluck, BOOM?
A chicken in a minefield!

What did Mr and Mrs Chicken call
their baby?
Egg.

Where do you find a dog with no legs?
Right where you left him!

What did the turtle say to the tortoise?
Shell be right, mate!

What do you call an elephant in a
phone box?
Stuck.

What do you get when you mix a
Tyrannosaurus with explosives?
Dino-mite!

How do you know if you're in bed with
an elephant?
The pillow smells like peanuts.

What's the difference between the sky
and a lion with a thorn in its paw?
One pours with rain and the other
roars with pain!

Why do elephants never forget?
What do they have to remember?

What do you call a bear with no ears?
A 'b'!

What's black and white and black and

white and black and white and black and white and black and white and black and white and black and white and black and white and black and white and white and black and

white and barks?

101 Dalmatians!

Where are foals born?
Horsepital.

Did you hear about the dog that lost
its temper?
It hit the woof.

What do you call a cow riding a skateboard?
A cow-tastrophe waiting to happen.

Why are intelligent ducks like comedians?
They're always making wisequacks.

What do dogs and trees have in common?
Bark.

How do apes protect themselves
against invaders?
They organise gorilla campaigns.

Where do rabbits go to have their fur styled?
The local haredresser.

Why do old snakes complain?
Fangs aren't what they used to be.

What is a slug?
A snail with a housing problem.

What did one elephant say to the
other elephant?
Have you seen my tail?

Why are elephant herds in such demand
at employment agencies?
They are really good at multi-tusking.

What did the duck say
to the comedian after
the show?
That really quacked
me up!

What's black and white and eats like
a horse?
A zebra.

What kind of printer does a pig use?
An oinkjet!

What did the disapproving mother elephant
say to her little one?
Tusk, tusk!

Why is an octopus always ready for a fight?
It's well armed.

What do you call a
sleeping bull?
A bulldozer.

Which dog is always
ready for a fight?
A boxer.

What did the frog say when he went to the library?
Read it, read it, read it!

Did you hear about the sad duckling who tucked his head into his feathers?
He felt down.

What do you call a group of rabbits hopping backwards?
A receding hareline!

Why did Mrs Fly fly?
Because Mr Spider spied 'er.

What did the young spider want to be when she grew up?
A web designer.

Where do frogs keep their money?
In riverbanks!

What animal should
you never play cards with?
A cheetah.

Why did the dog sit
under the tree?
Because he didn't want
to be a hot dog.

What did the mosquito
say to his friend?
Do you want to go out for a bite?

How did the dog stop the DVD player?
He used the PAWS button.

There were ten cats in a boat. One
jumped out. How many were left?
None, they were all copycats.

What kind of birds live in tin trees?
Toucans!

Where do herds of wildebeest migrate
to every year?
Gnu pastures.

Hickory dickory dock,
three mice ran up the clock,
the clock struck one,
but the other two got away with
minor injuries.

Classroom Wisecracks

What kind of teachers will we never run
out of?
Maths teachers, because they always
multiply.

Why was the teacher cross-eyed?
Because she couldn't control her pupils!

What's the friendliest school?
Hi school.

What do you call that great feeling of
satisfaction you get when you finish
your homework?
The aftermath.

Joshua: Teacher, I'd like to bring my five dogs to school.
Teacher: But what about the noise and the mess?
Joshua: Oh, they won't mind.

What kind of school do you have to drop out of to graduate?
Sky-diving school.

Sophie: Teacher, teacher, I've just swallowed a bone!
Teacher: Are you choking?
Sophie: No, I'm serious.

Teacher: Johnny, if you had five Mars Bars and Stevie asked for two, how many would you have left?
Johnny: Five.

Where do cows go to study?
Moo-niversity.

Which is the best hand to write with?
It's probably better to write with a pen.

What 11-letter word does everybody
always pronounce incorrectly?
Incorrectly.

Teacher: Mark, give me a sentence
starting with the letter 'I'.
Mark: I is ...
Teacher: No, Mark. It's 'I am', not 'I is'.
Try again.
Mark: Okay. I am the ninth letter of
the alphabet.

What made Kevin Kea go
around and around and
around and around and
around the playground?
He lost his marbles!

A Year 5 class goes on an excursion on the ferry across the Cook Strait to Picton. When they arrive at the ferry terminal, the teacher gives everyone a talk on the safety rules. She is sure everyone will be safe except for naughty Nathan, who has been mucking around through the entire safety lecture.

'Nathan!' yells the teacher. 'This is very important. What do you yell if you see one of your fellow students go over the side of the Interislander?'

To the teacher's surprise, Nathan replies, 'Man overboard!'

'Okay then,' says the teacher, suspecting a lucky guess. 'What do you yell if your teacher goes over the side of the Interislander?'

'Hooray!'

Who is Kiri Kiwi's best
friend at school?
Her princi-pal.

Tommy Tuatara: Why did
you bring your computer
to school, Kevin?
Kevin Kea : My mum told me to bring an
awesome apple for Miss Smith!

What did the kid say when the teacher asked
who kept putting boogers on her chair?
S'not me!

Why did Kevin Kea give the teacher
a C sharp?
It was a note from his parents!

Kevin Kea: How did you go in your test?
Pippa Pukeko: Well, it was watery.
Kevin Kea: What do you mean?
Pippa Pukeko: My results were under C level!

Kiri Kiwi: I didn't understand that test. Why were all the questions from before I was born?

Kevin Kea: It was a history test …

Teacher: How many sides does Kiri Kiwi's nest have?

Pupil: Two – the inside and the outside!

Teacher: Pippa, do you know when the Great Depression was?

Pippa: Yes, when I got my last haircut!

What is that tree in the playground, Joshua?

Elemen-tree!

What kind of bee loves going to school?

A spelling bee.

What bird loves singing class?
A hummingbird.

What kind of school do magicians go to?
Charm school!

Teacher: What's that sound I can hear
from the gym? It sounds like music.
Kiri Kiwi: The sports teacher told Keith
to go get a ball. I guess Keith thought he
meant the dancing kind!

What sort of end-of-school dance do
rabbits go to?
A hare-ball.

Intergalactic Giggles

Why did the alien throw out all its clothes when it landed in Auckland?
It was out-o'-space!

What kind of music can you hear in space?
A Nep-tune.

Did you hear about Marama, the astronomer who got knocked out?
She saw stars.

What did the hungry spaceman say to his co-pilot?
Pass the astro-nuts.

How do angels answer the phone?
Halo?

What do shooting stars say when they are
introduced to one another?
Nice to meteor!

What do US astronauts do after a busy
morning in space?
They go out to launch!

Why were the US astronauts never around?
They kept going out to launch!

What do black holes eat for dinner?
Star-ghetti.

How do you get an astronaut's baby to sleep?
Rocket.

Why was the alien afraid?
It was surrounded by shooting stars!

Why was the kiwi on the red carpet?
Because it wanted to watch the stars
come out.

Why was the moon
party dull?
Because it had
no atmosphere!

Why are there only 18 letters
in the alphabet?
Because ET went home in a UFO and the
CIA went after him!

What sort of dance do aliens do?
The moon walk!

Why was the alien cross?
Because he forgot change for the
parking meteor!

What do you call a wizard in outer space?
A flying sorcerer.

Kiwi: Why are you throwing vegetables in the sky, dear?
Chick: Because I wanted to cook dinner for you in the Pot!

Why wasn't the moon hungry?
Because it was full.

What sort of gymnastics are aliens good at?
The moon beam.

How do you know the sun is clean?
It always shines.

What did the alien say to the garden?
Take me to your weeder.

Famous Funnies

Why was Cinderella so bad at sport?
Because she had a pumpkin for a coach
and she ran away from the ball.

What do Kermit the Frog and Alexander
the Great have in common?
The same middle name!

What's the easiest way to get on
New Zealand TV?
Sit next to the aerial!

What did Snow White say while she
waited for photos?
Someday my prints will come.

What is a pig's
favourite superhero?
The Oinkredible Hulk.

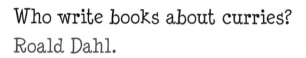

What would Bob the Builder
be if he wasn't a builder?
Bob.

Who write books about curries?
Roald Dahl.

What's Winnie the Pooh's middle name?
The.

What do you call Batman and Robin after
they've been run over?
Flatman and Ribbon!

Why is Cinderella so bad at soccer?
She keeps running away from the ball!

How does the Easter Bunny stay so fit?
He gets lots of eggs-ercise with
hare-obics!

Which conqueror of the ancient world
invented fireplaces?
Alexander the Grate.

Who swears, and is scared of wolves?
Little Rude Riding Hood.

Which great French military leader fell
to bits?
Napoleon Bones-apart!

Which famous pharaoh was seriously
overweight?
Two-Tonne Carmen.

What do you call James Bond in the
bath?
Bubble-o-7!

Which famous queen suffered badly
from measles?
Mary, Queen of Spots.

Which famous philosopher loved
French fries?
Plato Chips.

Do Santa's reindeer enjoy his jokes?
Yes. He sleighs 'em.

In Santa's sleigh team, who is the most
ill-mannered?
Rude Alf, the red-nosed reindeer.

How does Santa stop his sleigh?
He just pulls on the rein, dear.

Why is there never a drought where
Santa lives?
There's always plenty of rain, dear.

Does Santa enjoy being king of the
North Pole?
Yes, he likes his reign, dear.

Which famous movies involve lots of
climbing?
Lord of the Rungs and *Stair Wars*.

Which Wild West hero had a throat
spasm problem?
Wild Bill Hiccup.

Did Moby Dick enjoy the party?
He had a whale of a time.

Which Wild West outlaw was a bit of
a goat?
Billy the Kid.

Which Wild West frontiersman had a
very short hairstyle?
Davy Crewcut.

Why did Piglet look inside the toilet?
Because he was looking for Pooh!

What is the name of the fishy spy?
James Pond.

Which vegetable became a
rock 'n' roll superstar?
Elvis Parsley.

Road-Wise Rib-Ticklers

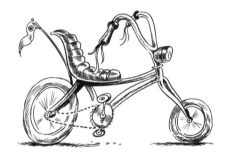

Why can a bicycle not stand alone?
It is two tired.

What happened to the wooden car with the wooden engine and wooden tyres?
It wooden go.

Two police officers are driving a car. One officer puts on the siren and asks the other officer to check whether it's working. He answers 'Yes ... no ... yes ... no ... yes ... no ... yes ... no ...'

What do you give an unwell car?
A fuel injection.

How does the queen
get around her palace?
She's throne.

What flies and smells bad?
A smellycopter.

How do rabbits fly?
By hare plane.

How do Kiwi pilots undress for bed?
They prepare for take-off.

How did the car get a flat tyre?
There was a fork in the road.

What's a fjord?
A Norwegian car.

What's the last thing that goes through a
bee's mind when he hits the windshield?
His bottom!

What do bees do if they don't want
to drive?
Go to the buzz stop.

What do you call music coming out
of a car?
A cartune!

What did the traffic light say to the other
traffic light?
Excuse me, I'm changing.

What flies and wobbles?
A jellycopter.

What happens when a cane toad
breaks down?
It gets toad away.

Kiri: Keith! Call me a taxi!
Keith: Certainly, Kiri. You're a taxi.

Policeman: Did you know you were
driving at 125 kilometres an hour?
Driver: Impossible. I've only been driving
for five minutes.

What did the dog say as it admired the
front of the big ship?
Bow! Wow!

Where does an elephant keep its luggage?
In its trunk.

How do fleas travel?
They itch-hike.

Gross Gags

What animal goes 'aaa'?
A sheep with a blocked nose.

What did one toilet say to the other?
You look a little flushed.

How do you make a handkerchief dance?
Put some boogie in it.

Why did the pukeko
bring toilet paper to
the party?
Because he was a
party pooper!

If people point to their mouths when they're hungry and their wrists when they want the time, why don't they point to their bums when they need the bathroom?

What's green, sticky and smells like eucalyptus?
Koala spew.

What's green and hangs from tall trees?
Giraffe snot.

What's yellow and smells of bananas?
Monkey vomit.

Which two New Zealand cities are the stinkiest?
Rottenrua and Smellington

If you're a New Zealander in the kitchen, a New Zealander in the lounge room and a New Zealander in the bedroom, what are you in the toilet?
European.

Did you hear about the nose that was badly behaved?
It was very, very snotty.

Two blokes go into a hotel toilet. One is in the navy and the other is in the army. When they are done, the navy bloke goes to the sink and starts to wash his hands, while the army bloke goes to walk straight out the door.

The navy bloke calls after the army bloke, 'The navy teaches us to wash our hands!'

The army bloke calls back, 'The army teaches us not to pee on ours!'

Which big animal needs a bath?
A smellyphant.

What do you call a smelly fairy?
Stinkerbell.

What's a face race?
It's a feature race.

Is the face race a new idea?
No, it's been happening for ears and ears.

Did Jack enter the face race?
Yes, his nose was running.

Did Jill enter the face race?
Yes, her eyes were running.

Why was Jack disqualified from the
face race?
He was too cheeky.

Was Jack upset?
No, he took it on the chin.

Who won the face race?
Jill. She was blinking fast.

Will the face race continue?
Definitely! There will be lots of new faces
next year.

Will Jack compete again next year?
Who nose?

Why do gorillas have big noses?
Because they have big fingers.

What did the lazy right hand think to itself?
I'd better knuckle down.

What do you call a sheep in a rainstorm?
A wet blanket.

Why was the hand proud of itself?
It had made a good fist of things.

What do your hands need so they can visit
your arms?
Two-wrist visas.

What did the snake say to her young son?
Stop crying and viper your nose.

Do hands enjoy life?
Thumb do and thumb don't.

What's invisible and smells like chocolate?
Easter bunny farts!

What's invisible, noisy and
smells like bananas?
A monkey burp!

Did you hear about the octopus that
became a soldier?
It was well-armed.

Which tree has a sore mouth?
Red gum.

Why did the surgeon think the patient
was hilarious?
He had her in stitches.

How can you tell when a moth farts?
It flies straight for a few seconds.

What did the finger say to the thumb?
I'm in glove with you.

What's the difference between flies
and cockroaches?
Flies are easier to get out from
between your teeth.

Did you hear about the bloke who took five days off work because of a chest cold?
He had a wee cough.

What do you find up a clean nose?
Fingerprints.

Why do mother birds puke in their babies' mouths?
They want to send them out with a hot breakfast.

Why did the one-handed person cross the road?
To get to the second-hand shop.

Doctor, doctor. I keep thinking I am a dustbin.
Rubbish!

Why did the turkey stop eating her
dinner?
She was already stuffed.

What do magicians like to keep up their
sleeves?
Their arms!

Why did the hand feel safe in a glove?
It was out of arm's way.

Why are hippies so useful?
Because they help swing your leggies!

Knock, Knocks

Knock, knock.
Who's there?
Howard.
Howard who?
Howard I know!

Knock, knock.
Who's there?
Eileen.
Eileen who?
Eileen on you,
you lean on me!

Knock, knock.
Who's there?
Archie!
Archie who?
Bless you!

Knock, knock.
Who's there?
Ben.
Ben who?
Ben knocking so long my hand hurts!

Knock, knock.
Who's there?
Claire.
Claire who?
Claire the way, I'm coming in!

Knock, knock.
Who's there?
Hugo.
Hugo who?
Hugo this way, I go that way.

Knock, knock.
Who's there?
Amos.
Amos who?
Amosquito just bit me!

Knock, knock.
Who's there?
Andy.
Andy who?
Andy just bit me again!

Knock, knock.
Who's there?
The Interrupting Sheep.
The Interrupting Sh—
Baaa!

Knock, knock.
Who's there?
Emma.
Emma who?
Emma cracking you up?

Knock, knock.
Who's there?
Phillip.
Phillip who?
Phillip my lunch box, I'm hungry today!

Knock, knock.
Who's there?
Keith.
Keith who?
Keith me, thweet heart!

Would you miss me if I left tomorrow?
Yes
Would you miss me if I left next week?
Yes
Would you miss me if I left next year?
Yes
Knock, knock.
Who's there?
Oh, you have forgotten me already!

Knock, knock.
Who's there?
Sarah.
Sarah who?
Sarah reason you're
not laughing?

Knock, knock.
Who's there?
Max.
Max who?
Max no difference to you, just let me in.

Knock, knock.
Who's there?
Lettuce.
Lettuce who?
Lettuce come in to your party, it's boring
out here!

Knock, knock.
Who's there?
Statue.
Statue who?
Statue, bro?

Knock, knock.
Who's there?
Noah.
Noah who?
Noah good place to find more jokes?

Make A Donation
To Cure Kids

TURNING RESEARCH INTO HOPE

It's easy to contribute to Cure Kids
programmes — your dollars go towards
putting a smile on a child's face.
We need all the help you can give —
so tell your family, friends and the
people you work with to visit the
Cure Kids website www.curekids.org.nz
to make an online donation, or send
in the slip on the reverse page.

DONATION FORM

Copy and post or email to
Cure Kids, PO Box 90907, Auckland 1142
Email: info@curekids.org.nz

Enclosed is my donation   **$**

☐ Cash   ☐ Cheque (please make payable to Cure Kids)
☐ Credit Card (see below)

....

Please debit my credit card

(Please tick)   ☐ Bankcard   ☐ MasterCard
                     ☐ Visa   ☐ American Express

Card Number

Expiry Date   [   ] / [   ]

Name on Card

Please sign

....

First name

Last name

Company

Address

Suburb

City

Postcode

Email

Phone

Thank you for your support.
Do you wish to receive information in future from Cure Kids? Yes/No
Donations of $5 or more are tax deductible.